D0609547

I am growing and changing

Bobbie Kalman

 Crabtree Publishing Company

www.crabtreebooks.com

Created by Bobbie Kalman

Author and Editor-in-Chief
Bobbie Kalman

Educational consultants
Joan King
Reagan Miller
Elaine Hurst

Editors
Reagan Miller
Joan King
Kathy Middleton

Proofreader
Crystal Sikkens

Design
Bobbie Kalman
Katherine Berti

Photo research
Bobbie Kalman

Production coordinator
Katherine Berti

Prepress technician
Katherine Berti

Photographs by Shutterstock

Library and Archives Canada Cataloguing in Publication

Kalman, Bobbie, 1947-
      I am growing and changing / Bobbie Kalman.

(My world)
ISBN 978-0-7787-9422-6 (bound).--ISBN 978-0-7787-9466-0 (pbk.)
      4430 7469 8/10
      1. Children--Growth--Juvenile literature.
I. Title. II. Series: My world (St. Catharines, Ont.)

QP84.K34 2010   j612.6'5   C2009-906058-2

Library of Congress Cataloging-in-Publication Data

Kalman, Bobbie.
 I am growing and changing / Bobbie Kalman.
      p. cm. -- (My world)
  ISBN 978-0-7787-9466-0 (pbk. : alk. paper) -- ISBN 978-0-7787-9422-6
(reinforced library binding : alk. paper)
 1. Human growth--Juvenile literature. I. Title. II. Series.

  QP84.K35 2010
  612--dc22

                                                             2009040959

Crabtree Publishing Company

www.crabtreebooks.com   1-800-387-7650

Printed in China/122009/CT20091009

Published in Canada
Crabtree Publishing
616 Welland Ave.
St. Catharines, Ontario
L2M 5V6

Published in the United States
Crabtree Publishing
PMB 59051
350 Fifth Avenue, 59th Floor
New York, New York 10118

Published in the United Kingdom
Crabtree Publishing
Maritime House
Basin Road North, Hove
BN41 1WR

Published in Australia
Crabtree Publishing
386 Mt. Alexander Rd.
Ascot Vale (Melbourne)
VIC 3032

Words to know

baby

baby crawling

baby teeth

riding a tricycle

toddler walking

3

I am a baby.
I was born today.

I am two days old.
I sleep a lot!

I am a baby.
I am three weeks old.
I have no teeth.

I am four months old.
I can grab my feet and roll.
I am growing and changing.

I am eight months old.
I am **crawling** now.
I have **baby teeth**.

I am one year old.
I am walking now.
I am a **toddler**.
I am growing
and changing.

I am two years old.
I can play and talk.
I am growing
and changing.

I am four years old.
I am riding a **tricycle** now.
I can ride it fast!

I am five years old.

I go to school.

I am learning to read and write.

I can do many things.
I can learn anything!
I am growing and changing.

Activity

When did you
start crawling?

When did you
start walking?

When did you start school?
Have you lost
your baby teeth yet?
How else
are you changing?

Everything changes

There are changes in the weather, the days of the week, months, years, and in people. Ask the children what changes have happened to them since they were born. What changes were there in their bodies—such as height, weight, color and length of hair, and when they got their first baby teeth and when they started losing them.

Have them create timelines for each year of their lives. Ask them to make a list of all the skills they have learned since they were born.

Baby you!

Invite each child to bring in a baby picture. Tell the children not to allow anyone else to see their pictures. Collect the photographs and post them on a bulletin board. Number each photo. On a sheet of paper, ask the children to write down the numbers and, beside each number, ask them to write the name of the student that they think is in the photo. After they are finished, reveal the names of the babies in the photos. Ask them how many of their matches were correct. This fun activity demonstrates that growth changes how children look.

Really big changes!

Show children a book about caterpillar to butterfly metamorphosis and ask them how their growth and changes are the same as, or different from, the growth of a butterfly. Can they grow into beautiful butterflies, too?

Guided Reading: J

16